THE
ZIKA VIRUS

BY SUE BRADFORD EDWARDS

CONTENT CONSULTANT

Sahotra Sarkar
Department of Integrative Biology
University of Texas at Austin

Essential Library

An Imprint of Abdo Publishing | abdopublishing.com

abdopublishing.com

Published by Abdo Publishing, a division of ABDO, PO Box 398166, Minneapolis, Minnesota 55439. Copyright © 2017 by Abdo Consulting Group, Inc. International copyrights reserved in all countries. No part of this book may be reproduced in any form without written permission from the publisher. Essential Library™ is a trademark and logo of Abdo Publishing.

Printed in the United States of America, North Mankato, Minnesota
092016
012017

**THIS BOOK CONTAINS
RECYCLED MATERIALS**

Cover Photo: Felipe Dana/AP Images
Interior Photos: Shutterstock Images, 4–5, 32; Kyodo/AP Images, 7; Ricardo Mazalan/AP Images, 11, 24, 46; Red Line Editorial, 14–15, 49; Cynthia Goldsmith/CDC, 16–17; David Scharf/Science Source, 20; Arnulfo Franco/AP Images, 27; Ricardo Funari/Brazil Photos/LightRocket/Getty Images, 29; Isaac Kasamani/AFP/Getty Images, 30–31; Pascal Goetgheluck/Science Source, 36; Piotr Gatlik/Shutterstock Images, 38–39; Dr. Tony Brain/Science Source, 50–51; Felipe Dana/AP Images, 55, 60–61; Leo Correa/AP Images, 58; Andre Penner/AP Images, 63, 69, 97; Monica Schroeder/Science Source, 66; Danica Coto/AP Images, 72–73, 83; Esteban Felix/AP Images, 75; Lynne Sladky/AP Images, 79; Richard J. Green/Science Source, 86–87; Mark Lennihan/AP Images, 89; Scott Olson/Getty Images, 92; Evan Oto/Science Source, 94

Editor: Arnold Ringstad
Series Designer: Maggie Villaume

Publisher's Cataloging-in-Publication Data

Names: Edwards, Sue Bradford, author.
Title: The zika virus / by Sue Bradford Edwards.
Description: Minneapolis, MN : Abdo Publishing, 2017. | Series: Special reports |
    Includes bibliographical references and index.
Identifiers: LCCN 2016945411 | ISBN 9781680784008 (lib. bdg.) |
    ISBN 9781680797534 (ebook)
Subjects: LCSH: Zika virus disease--Juvenile literature | Epidemiology--Juvenile
    literature. | Disease outbreaks--Juvenile literature.
Classification: DDC 616.9--dc23
LC record available at http://lccn.loc.gov/2016945411

CONTENTS

CHAPTER ONE

TAKING ZIKA
SERIOUSLY

In late 2015, Jade Coelho de Miranda was a 20-year-old student at the Federal University of the State of Rio de Janeiro in Brazil. She often visited a park near her school. The park swarmed with mosquitoes, but at first she did not worry about them. Then she developed a red rash over much of her body.

The rash worried her, so she told her father about it. He encouraged her to check into the hospital. After examining and testing de Miranda, doctors determined she was infected with the Zika virus. She was soon experiencing the standard symptoms of Zika. She developed muscle pain and a fever. Then she started having trouble moving her hands. They felt as if they were frozen in place. Even her eyes felt irritated.

Mosquitoes' ability to spread diseases makes them among the planet's most dangerous animals.

Soon de Miranda's father also became sick. A Zika-carrying mosquito had bitten him too, but his illness was not limited to the common Zika symptoms. For him the Zika virus led to Guillain-Barré syndrome, a rare disorder in which the body's own immune system attacks the nerves. He experienced extreme weakness and tingling in his fingers, toes, ankles, and wrists that lasted for three months.

Both de Miranda and her father recovered, but they were far from the only victims of the Zika virus. It did not stop in Brazil. By 2016, the virus had spread worldwide. As it appeared in one country after another, scientists began noticing disturbing trends. Some pregnant women who

"CASES LIKE MY DAD'S WORRY ME THE MOST, AS ZIKA HAS A DIFFERENT EFFECT ON EACH PERSON. SOME PEOPLE MIGHT DEVELOP A RARE SYNDROME LIKE HE DID."[1]

— JADE COELHO DE MIRANDA, SPEAKING ABOUT THE GUILLAIN-BARRÉ SYNDROME HER FATHER DEVELOPED AS A RESULT OF HAVING THE ZIKA VIRUS

MOSQUITOES AND DISEASE

Mosquitoes bite because they feed on blood. The protein in blood is necessary for many female mosquitoes to produce eggs. A mosquito can pick up viruses or other disease-carrying organisms from the blood of the animal on which it is feeding. It can then transmit the disease to another animal, or even to another species. Mosquitoes transmit a variety of diseases, including Zika, malaria, yellow fever, chikungunya, and dengue fever. Different types of mosquitoes transmit different diseases.

became infected with Zika were giving birth to children with major medical problems. Researchers scrambled to learn more about the link between the virus and these serious birth defects.

FROM UGANDA TO THE REST OF THE WORLD

The virus was discovered in 1945 in the Zika Forest of Uganda, a country in east Africa. In the Zika Forest, mosquitoes carrying the virus bit and infected local monkeys. Only rarely did the mosquitoes bite and infect humans. Over the following decades, health-care providers

The Zika Forest has been a site of virus research for decades.

and scientists found the virus in animals in other parts of Africa and in South and Southeast Asia. Before 2007, there had been only 14 confirmed cases of Zika in humans.[2]

Between 2007 and 2013, infected mosquitoes and infected people were found on one island after another throughout the Pacific Ocean. These islands included Yap island in the Federated States of Micronesia and various islands in French Polynesia. As the virus moved across the Pacific, more and more people got sick. Some, such as de Miranda's father, developed Guillain-Barré syndrome. Many others had only the typical Zika symptoms: fever, headache, and a variety of aches and pains.

Doctors and scientists realized how serious the Zika virus could be in early 2015, when it was confirmed to have reached the Americas. Between 3 and 4 million people in the Americas contracted the virus in just nine months. Many cases of the illness were mild, and most people recovered from them. But because there were now so many infections overall, the risk of birth defects and other neurological complications became apparent. It was estimated that among women who develop the virus during the first three months of their pregnancies, 1 in 100 will give birth to a baby with these issues.[3] By January 2016, approximately 4,000 children in the Americas had been born with Zika-related birth defects.[4]

PUBLIC HEALTH EMERGENCY

On February 1, 2016, the World Health Organization (WHO) declared the spread of the Zika virus a public health emergency of international concern. WHO director general Dr. Margaret Chan announced this state of emergency. "Local transmission has now been reported in 31 countries and territories in Latin America and the Caribbean," said Chan.[5]

Before making this announcement, she met with a committee of experts to assess whether the Zika outbreak met all the criteria for an emergency of international concern. Such an emergency must involve a problem that

VIRUSES AND BIRTH DEFECTS

The Zika virus is one of several viruses that can affect the brain of a developing infant. A fetus, or a developing embryo, does not have a fully formed immune system to fight off the Zika virus. As the virus grows and spreads, it interferes with the growth of cells in the fetus. It often affects the complex process of brain development. Virologist Kristen Bernard of the University of Wisconsin–Madison notes, "There are a lot of sensitive cells there that have to get to the right places at the right time."[6] Disruptions to this process, including those caused by the Zika virus, can lead to severe problems with the brain.

reaches epidemic proportions, affecting large numbers of people in a short time. It must cross national boundaries and threaten populations, meaning entire groups of people, such as pregnant women and their children. Solutions to this kind of an emergency can be found fastest when organizations pool their resources and work together. By declaring a public health emergency, the WHO would be able to coordinate research on this virus, particularly regarding its effect on pregnant women. The organization encouraged governments and nonprofit groups to help fund this research and begin the process of developing a vaccine against Zika.

PREVIOUS PATTERNS

Scientists and doctors were not certain what the eventual impact of the Zika virus would be, but they knew it would

Pregnant women in Brazil, Colombia, and other South American nations found themselves at the center of international attention during the Zika outbreak.

likely continue spreading. They believed it might follow

the pattern of a related virus called chikungunya. This virus

was first described in 1952 in Tanzania, a country on the

east coast of Africa. After this outbreak, researchers found

chikungunya throughout Africa and Asia, but the number

of people infected remained low. Then, in 1999 and 2000,

CHIKUNGUNYA

As with the Zika virus, chikungunya is typically transmitted by a mosquito bite. Most people who are infected with the virus show symptoms. The first symptom is often a rapid rise in body temperature. The second is joint pain. Many viruses cause aches and pains, but the joint pain in chikungunya is so severe patients often cannot stand up. They cannot even shake someone's hand because it is too painful. Although most patients recover fully and feel better in a week, in some cases the joint pain can linger for months. Fortunately, once a patient recovers from chikungunya, he or she is immune for life. In past outbreaks, approximately one in 1,000 cases has been fatal.[9]

a larger outbreak took place in Africa's Democratic Republic of the Congo. In 2004, outbreaks occurred in two villages in Kenya. Up to 75 percent of the people in the village contracted the virus.[7]

In December 2013, two cases of chikungunya were reported on Saint Martin, an island in the Caribbean Sea. These cases marked the first reports of local transmission in the Americas. Before this, travelers had returned to the Americas already sick from the virus. This was the first time someone had actually gotten the virus after being bitten by a mosquito in the Americas. From those two cases, the numbers of countries and people affected has continually grown. By April 2015, approximately 1.7 million suspected cases of chikungunya had been reported in 43 nations in North and South America.[8] "Chikungunya is an amazing virus," says Ann Powers, a virologist with the US Centers for Disease Control and Prevention (CDC). "It spreads incredibly fast and is very aggressive. In some communities, more than half the population gets sick."[10]

One of the nations in which chikungunya has found a home is the United States, where it has spread in Florida. Researchers believe the Zika virus may follow its lead. Zika is closely related to the chikungunya virus, and the same mosquito spreads it. As people around the world began worrying about the possible extent and severity of a widespread Zika outbreak, scientists worked to better understand the virus and its effects.

EPIDEMICS AND ENDEMIC DISEASES

Brazil's Minister of Health, Marcelo Castro, warned the Zika virus might be more than a passing epidemic. Castro says the Zika virus might represent an endemic disease, meaning it has become a permanent part of the Brazilian ecosystem and will never be driven out completely. Other mosquito-carried viruses that have already become endemic in the Americas include West Nile virus, yellow fever, dengue, and chikungunya.

FROM THE HEADLINES

MARSHALL
ISLANDS

KOSRAE
(MICRONESIA)

PAPUA
NEW GUINEA

SAMOA

FIJI

AMERICAN
SAMOA

NEW CALEDONIA

N
W E
S

COUNTRIES WITH
ACTIVE ZIKA TRANSMISSION,
MAY 2016

COUNTRIES WITH ACTIVE ZIKA TRANSMISSION, MAY 2016

When the WHO declared the Zika virus a public health emergency of international concern, news agencies worldwide recognized the virus as a pandemic, an epidemic crossing international borders. The virus had traveled across thousands of miles of open sea, from the western Pacific Ocean to South America. From there, it spread north into Central America and the Caribbean.

CHAPTER TWO

WHAT IS
ZIKA?

Similar to other viruses, the Zika virus is a microscopic particle much smaller than a human cell. Each particle consists of a single strand of ribonucleic acid (RNA) encased in protein. RNA is involved in the building of proteins inside living things. It also transmits genetic information. The RNA serves as a map for making more copies of the virus.

Viruses, including the Zika virus, are not considered living organisms under most definitions of being alive. This is because they cannot reproduce on their own. To reproduce, a virus particle attaches itself to a living host cell. Then the virus's genetic material enters the cell. The RNA travels to the host cell's nucleus, and the host cell builds multiple copies of the virus's RNA. The cell gives

Zika virus particles, *red*, are far too small to be seen with the naked eye.

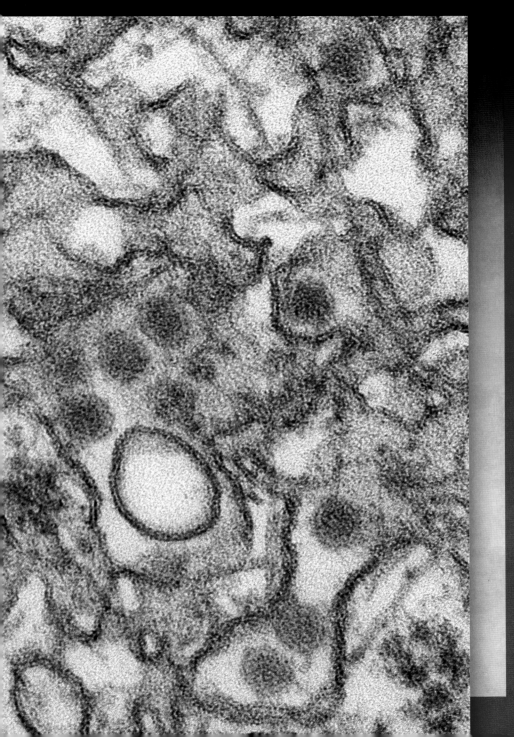

the RNA the same protein coating as the parent virus, and the newly built copies exit the cell to find new hosts.

The Zika virus is a flaviviridae virus. This name comes from the Latin word for "yellow," *flavus*, because the first flaviviridae virus discovered was the yellow fever virus. All flaviviridae viruses have a single strand of RNA coated with protein. Some of the viruses in this group can cause bleeding and encephalitis, or inflammation in the brain. The flaviviridae viruses include chikungunya, West Nile, yellow fever, and dengue fever. These viruses are commonly transmitted by arthropods, the group of animals that includes insects such as mosquitoes and ticks. The biting animals that transmit the virus from one host animal to another are known as vectors.

WHAT MAKES UP RNA?

RNA is made up of a string of molecules called nucleotides. Each nucleotide consists of a sugar, a phosphate, and one of four molecules called bases. These bases are cytosine, adenine, guanine, and uracil. The shape of RNA is complicated. The bases in a single strand of RNA pair together in a complex folding pattern scientists are still studying.

MALICIOUS MOSQUITOES

Viruses that have arthropod vectors are known as arboviruses. Ticks transmit some arboviruses, but the Zika virus is transmitted by mosquitoes. The most common vector is the *Aedes aegypti* mosquito.

Mosquitoes make ideal vectors because they sometimes feed on blood. *Aedes aegypti* mosquitoes become infected with the Zika virus when they bite an infected person or other infected animal, such as a monkey. The mosquito ingests the virus. Then the virus spreads through its digestive system to its circulatory system. From there, it travels to the mosquito's saliva. When an infected mosquito bites someone, it injects saliva into the bite. Mosquito saliva keeps the blood from clotting, allowing the insect to easily feed. It also spreads

DEFINING LIFE

Whether scientists are exploring a new biological particle or the reaches of space, they use the same criteria to judge whether something is alive. For something to be alive, it must grow and change over time. It must be responsive, meaning it reacts to its environment. In living organisms, chemical reactions take place at the cellular level. These reactions produce new cells and trigger the processes of growth and reproduction. Living organisms fuel these reactions with energy, usually provided by food or sunlight. The one thing living organisms do that viruses cannot is reproduce on their own. Viruses must occupy a host cell and use its reproductive mechanisms to duplicate themselves.

the virus into the bloodstream of the organism being bitten.

Aedes aegypti is not the only mosquito that can carry the Zika virus. The virus was first isolated from *Aedes africanus* mosquitoes in 1948. It has also been found in the closely related *Aedes albopictus*. But a mosquito can be infected with a virus and still be a poor vector. This happens when the virus is not present in the saliva at levels high enough to transmit the virus with a bite. During the outbreak, in 2016, scientists worked to determine which mosquitoes could both be infected by the virus and serve as effective vectors.

A VECTOR FOR MANY DISEASES

The *Aedes aegypti* mosquito is not only the vector for the Zika virus. It was originally known as the vector for yellow fever. Because of this, it is often called the yellow fever mosquito. It is also the vector for the dengue virus, the chikungunya virus, and the West Nile virus. Scientists believe it may also be a vector for the Venezuelan equine encephalitis virus.

Only female mosquitoes feed on blood and spread disease.

MORE TO THE
STORY

WHERE DO MOSQUITOES LIVE?

Some mosquitoes are dangerous vectors not only because of the viruses they transmit, but also because of how closely they come into contact with human beings. *Aedes aegypti* originally lived in remote forests, but for hundreds of years it has lived side-by-side with people. This arrangement works well for the mosquitoes. People serve not only as blood sources, but they also provide water in which the mosquitoes can lay their eggs. *Aedes aegypti* mosquitoes will lay eggs in any water-filled container in or outside someone's home, even toilets. It is this proximity to people that makes the *Aedes aegypti* mosquito a dangerous vector. A mosquito that lives only in dense forests, deep swamps, or other areas far from human contact would pose little risk simply because it is not near humans, even if it could act as a vector.

SYMPTOMS

Many people infected with Zika never know they have contracted it or are capable of spreading it to others. Only one in five people infected with the virus gets sick enough to show any symptoms. Common Zika virus symptoms are similar to those for many other viruses and include fever, rash, joint pain, and red eyes.

Fevers occur because the immune system is trying to fight off the infection. Most chemical reactions, including those that occur during the building of cells, have an ideal temperature range. This is the range at which the reactions most easily take place. The fever raises the body's temperature beyond the ideal range for cell reproduction. This, in turn, slows down the rate of infection. With the virus reproducing more slowly, the person's immune system can more easily eliminate it.

Other symptoms are caused by the infection itself. Viruses invading muscle tissue cause aches and pains. When viruses exit mucus cells, they rupture the cells and fluid enters the nasal passages, resulting in a runny nose. Viruses infecting the cells in the throat lead to a sore

throat. The symptoms for the Zika virus are so similar to those of dengue fever that many doctors initially diagnose their patients with the more common dengue virus.

The fact that so few people infected with Zika have serious symptoms can make the disease even more difficult to diagnose. This difficulty helps the virus spread. Patients may not even seek medical help, instead deciding to simply rest and heal on their own.

DIAGNOSIS

When the earliest Zika patients went to the doctor, there were two ways to test them for the virus. In a reverse transcription-polymerase chain reaction (PCR), the lab tests the patient's blood for pieces of the virus's genetic material. The problem with this test is it works only while the virus is

TESTING BLOOD FOR VIRUSES

When testing patients' blood for the Zika virus, sometimes the blood is tested in batches called mini-pools. Blood from three or more people is combined and run through one test. If the test comes back negative for the virus, then no more tests need to be done. The doctors know that none of the people have the virus. If this test comes back positive, blood from each of the people is tested again to find out who has the virus. Mini-pools are used when large numbers of people must be tested because it is cheaper to run one test than it is to run three or more. The disadvantage to testing pooled blood is that very low levels of a virus may not be detected in the combined sample, especially if only one person in the group has the virus.

A rash is among the common symptoms of Zika virus.

still in the blood. This means it can detect the virus for only approximately five days after the person is infected. After this five-day period, the virus can be found in saliva or semen. Scientists are still studying where it can be found in the human body and how it might be transmitted from one person to another.

The other test for the Zika virus is the Zika MAC-ELISA. This test does not look for the actual virus or pieces of its genetic material. Instead, it looks for the antibodies the immune system uses to fight the virus. This test can find the antibodies starting five days after infection. It can continue to detect them for up to 12 weeks after the infection.[2] It is cheaper and faster than the PCR technique, two factors that are important when local health centers and hospitals must test large numbers of patients for possible infection.

Researchers later developed a third test. The first step in this test is to cause the virus in the blood, if present, to reproduce. Because a larger sample is easier to detect, it makes the test more accurate. Then blood from the amplified sample is applied to a paper card. These hand-sized cards contain freeze-dried proteins, ribosomes,

A ZIKA CD   U ZIKA CD
CT: Undete   CT Undete

9596   POS QC
B U ZIKA CD   U ZIKA
CT: Undete   CT: 22.76

9599
C U ZIKA CD
CT: Undete

9602
D U ZIKA CD
CT: Undete

9603
E U ZIKA CD
CT: Undete

9604
F U ZIKA CD

Computer readouts can be used to show the results of blood tests for Zika.

and nucleic acids. They react to the Zika virus in the blood and change color. These changes can be seen by the human eye or detected using a special reader. This test is more accurate than previous tests because unlike them, it can distinguish between the dengue fever virus and the Zika virus. The test can be completed in approximately 30 minutes.[3] Because the proteins and other biological components have been freeze-dried, the cards can be stored at room temperature. This makes it easier for clinics in places with unreliable electricity to use this test.

One of the most significant concerns with Zika is that few people carrying the virus will be tested. Only 20 percent of all infected people show symptoms, and those who live in underdeveloped or impoverished areas may be less likely to visit a doctor even if they do show symptoms.[4] Because of these factors, many people are contagious without knowing it.

People in rural areas of Brazil often receive health care in small clinics or even in their own homes.

CHAPTER THREE

DISCOVERING ZIKA

S cientists discovered the Zika virus in the 1940s when they were researching the mosquitoes that carry yellow fever. They built a platform in the canopy of a tree in Uganda's Zika Forest. Scientists George Dick, Stuart Kitchen, and Alexander Haddow placed a rhesus monkey in a cage on top of the platform and waited to see if the monkey would get sick. On April 18, 1947, Rhesus 766 developed a fever.

When the monkey was still running a fever two days later, it was taken to a laboratory in the Ugandan town of Entebbe. Serum, an amber-colored liquid separated from the monkey's blood, was injected into laboratory mice. After ten days, all of the mice had gotten sick. When the scientists looked for the virus that had made

When researchers entered the Zika Forest in 1947, they were not expecting to find a new virus.

the mice sick, they did not see the yellow fever virus they had expected to find. Instead, they found a new virus.

Scientists typically inject serum into mice to create a controlled experiment. The scientists know exactly when the mice were exposed to the virus, and the researchers know the mice were not exposed to other viruses. They can chart the rate at which the mice fall sick and where the virus is found in the mice: blood, saliva, or brain. Generating an infection in lab mice allows scientists to observe the infection and responses to treatment.

Rhesus monkeys are native to Asia, but they are used for research around the world.

In January 1948, the researchers, who were still studying yellow fever, entered the forest to find the mosquitoes that transmitted the virus. They captured a variety of mosquitoes and took them back to the laboratory. They knew one type of mosquito they had captured, *Aedes africanus*, could transmit yellow fever. They collected these mosquitoes and refrigerated them. The mosquitoes were then ground into a solution that was injected into a group of laboratory mice. After seven days, the mice grew sick. From the mice, the scientists isolated the same virus that had been found in Rhesus 766. They named the virus after the forest in which it was found.

AEDES AFRICANUS

Aedes africanus is found throughout Africa. It lives in forested areas, laying eggs in holes in trees, stumps, and bamboo, as well as in containers of various kinds. Chikungunya and Rift Valley fever viruses have also been isolated from this mosquito, although it is not yet known whether the mosquito can serve as an effective vector for them.

A HUMAN CASE

Naming the virus was not the end of the work performed by Haddow, Kitchen, and Dick. They also tested the blood of 99 people in Uganda. In six of these people, they found antibodies for Zika virus. These proteins told the scientists these six people had once been infected by the virus and successfully fought it off. None of them showed any signs of being sick when their blood was tested.

The first human case of Zika in which active symptoms of the virus were observed occurred in 1964 when David Simpson, one of Dick's students, was studying the virus in Uganda and got sick. He had been in the country for two and a half months working with the virus in the lab. Simpson developed a pink rash that initially covered his body, face, neck, and upper arms. Eventually, it spread to his arms and legs and even onto the palms of his hands and the soles of his feet. Although the rash did not itch, it lasted for five days. Simpson noted he did not feel sick and was not

BEYOND ANIMAL TESTING

Occasionally scientists will go beyond using animals to experiment on actual human beings. In 1954, scientist William Bearcroft decided to see whether he could replicate Zika virus symptoms in himself. Mice had gotten sick when injected with serum from a sick child, and Bearcroft wondered whether he would develop the symptoms, too. He injected material from the brain of a sick mouse into his arm. In less than eight hours, he had developed the same fever and headache as the sick child. When he allowed *Aedes aegypti* mosquitoes to feed on his blood, five days after he had gotten sick, he did not find the virus. Scientists now believe he probably waited too long. The virus was likely either no longer in his blood or was there in such low levels that the test missed it.

34

suffering from the crippling aches and pains that often accompanied similar mosquito-carried viruses. Simpson injected a group of laboratory mice with his blood. When the mice got sick, he tested a virus he isolated from their brains against a variety of known infections. He discovered it was the Zika virus.

AFRICA AND ASIA

Scientists wondered where else this virus might be infecting animals and people. To find out, they tested human blood in Africa. Between 1951 and 1981, doctors found evidence of the virus in the serum of people throughout Africa, including residents of Nigeria, Tanzania, Egypt, Sierra Leon, Gabon, and the Central African Republic. During this same time, scientists were also testing *Aedes aegypti*. They found infected mosquitoes in the eastern African nation of Cote d'Ivoire. From 1971 to 1975, doctors tested people in Nigeria. In one test, they found 40 percent of the people they tested previously had the virus.[1] Some of the children who had the infection showed no symptoms. Others had fevers, headaches, and body pain. Birth defects were not observed.

Capturing and studying mosquitoes are key to learning more about the viruses they carry.

At the same time, scientists were testing people and mosquitoes throughout Asia. They found people who had fought off the virus in India, Malaysia, the Philippines, Thailand, Vietnam, and Indonesia. In a 1952 study in India, 33 of the 196 people tested for the Zika virus had antibodies against it.[2] Scientists also discovered infected mosquitoes in Malaysia.

Scientists were learning more about Zika and where it existed, but the virus was not researched as thoroughly as it would have been if it were considered dangerous. Before 2007, medical professionals did not consider it a serious health risk. Relatively few human cases had been reported despite the fact that the virus was widespread in Africa, Southern Asia, and Southeast Asia. People with the virus rarely sought medical help. Perhaps because of the perceived low danger, only *Aedes africanus* and *Aedes aegypti* mosquitoes were studied in relation to the virus.

Following the outbreaks of 2015, many other mosquito species have been examined and found to carry the virus. However, carrying it and being an efficient vector for spreading it are not the same thing. By 2016, as the newly discovered neurological effects of the virus became apparent, scientists worked to fill in the gaps in Zika research.

"IT IS POSSIBLE THAT THERE COULD BE SEVERAL PEOPLE, OR SO MANY PEOPLE OUT THERE WITH THE ZIKA VIRUS INFECTION, BUT BECAUSE MANY PEOPLE DO NOT SEEK TREATMENT IN THE HOSPITALS, WE COULD BE MISSING OUT."[3]

— DR. JOHN KAYUMA, A MANAGER AT THE UGANDA LAB THAT TESTS FOR ZIKA VIRUS INFECTIONS, SPEAKING IN JANUARY 2016

CHAPTER FOUR

GUILLAIN-BARRÉ AND FRENCH POLYNESIA

n April and May 2007, people on Yap Island in the southwest Pacific Ocean started getting sick. They had rashes, joint pain, and red eyes. The sickest visited their doctors, who took blood and tested it for various viruses. Because the clinic had test kits for the dengue virus, doctors tested them for this infection. Three tests came back positive. Still, based on the symptoms, the doctors suspected something else was causing the infection. In June, the doctors found that samples from the patients contained RNA from the Zika virus. Eventually 180 people on the island fell ill.[1]

Global travel and trade enabled the spread of the Zika virus between remote Pacific islands.

MORE TO THE
STORY

DENGUE SYMPTOMS

Doctors often initially diagnose Zika patients with dengue fever because the symptoms caused by the two viruses are so similar. The most common symptoms of dengue fever are headaches, body pain, and a high fever. Other symptoms include a widespread rash, vomiting, and bleeding from the nose and gums. Zika's common symptoms include rashes, aches and pains, and red eyes. It can also cause fever, headache, and vomiting. If a patient has secondary symptoms of the Zika virus, such as fever and a headache, the illness closely resembles a dengue infection. A correct diagnosis is made even more difficult because Zika patients sometimes test positive for the dengue virus. This incorrect test result is called a false positive. Confusion also results from the fact that the Zika virus often appears in areas already affected by the dengue virus.

Experts paid close attention to the course of the infection on Yap Island. Until 2007, scientists and doctors had never found the Zika virus outside of Africa and Asia. In addition to being found someplace new, the virus had made more people than ever before sick enough to see their doctors. Before this outbreak, there had been only a handful of cases of people being actively sick from the virus. Even as the virus played out on Yap Island, no one was sick enough to stay in the hospital, and no one died. Still, it was the first time the virus had caused an extensive outbreak in a human population. Because this outbreak occurred on an island, doctors realized the virus could easily spread as people and goods moved between nations via travel or trade.

The mosquito scientists suspected spread the infection on Yap Island was *Aedes hensilli*. Researchers were unable to find the virus in any of the mosquitoes they tested, though of 12 mosquito types in their samples, *Aedes hensilli* was the most numerous. This same mosquito was also named the most likely vector for the transmission of dengue virus on the island.

ISLAND TO ISLAND

The presence of Zika on Yap Island was only the first step in the movement of the virus across the islands of the Pacific. Initially, the Zika virus was often confused with the dengue virus in French Polynesia. Doctors were familiar with dengue because it spread globally in the 1700s. However, doctors soon realized a different disease had to be at work. When a person is infected with dengue a second time, the disease is often more severe than the first infection. Many of the patients had already had dengue, and those with the new disease were not very sick.

The doctors at the Institut Louis Malardé in Tahiti, the most populous island in French Polynesia, were part of a program looking for mosquito-borne illnesses in the Pacific Islands. They knew the Zika virus had been found on

REPEATED DENGUE IS DEADLY

The first time a person is infected by the dengue virus, his or her body fights off the infection and antibodies are produced. These proteins recognize viruses a body has already fought off. They usually make it easier to fight off a virus the second or third time a person encounters it, but that is not how it works with the dengue virus. There are four strains of the dengue virus. If the patient has one strain the first time and one of the other three strains the second time, the antibodies actually make it easier for the virus to invade cells and spread.

MORE TO THE STORY

DENGUE HISTORY

Similar to the Zika virus, the dengue virus is spread by mosquitoes. However, its spread happened much earlier than Zika's. The earliest known case was recorded in a Chinese encyclopedia in 992 CE, but the dengue virus did not begin to spread worldwide until the 1700s. During this era, ships sailed the world carrying goods and people from one country to another. Port cities grew and became perfect feeding grounds for the *Aedes aegypti* mosquito. As the mosquito and virus spread to new areas, so did dengue fever epidemics. After World War II (1939–1945), when cities grew rapidly in Southeast Asia, doctors saw a new, deadlier form of the disease. They called it dengue hemorrhagic fever. The early symptoms of dengue hemorrhagic fever are the same as those for a dengue infection. But after several days, instead of getting better, the patient becomes irritated, unsettled, and sweaty. Tiny spots of blood appear on the skin and larger pools gather beneath the skin. The illness can be fatal if the patient goes into shock. Dengue continues to be among the most serious viral infections in tropical cities.

Yap Island, 5,000 miles (8,000 km) to the west, so they were ready to test their own patients for Zika. Soon the tests were coming back positive. Zika virus had been found in French Polynesia.

As doctors talked to their patients, they noted complaints about a symptom that had never before been associated with the Zika virus. People had ulcers, or open sores, in their mouths. Doctors wondered whether the virus was changing. They also recognized that as more people became infected, the presence of rarer symptoms would become more obvious.

GUILLAIN-BARRÉ SYNDROME

Approximately five weeks after getting sick with the Zika virus, some patients developed a neurological problem called Guillain-Barré syndrome. Doctors in French Polynesia normally see two cases of this disorder per year. From 2013 to 2014, they saw 42.[2]

People who develop Guillain-Barré usually have a viral infection several days or weeks prior to developing this rare syndrome. Doctors do not know why some patients develop this disorder whereas others do not. It is an autoimmune disease, meaning the patient's own immune system attacks the body. In this particular disorder, the immune system attacks the myelin sheath that covers the nerves. This covering speeds up transmissions along the nerves and allows the transmissions to travel farther. Because the body is attacking this covering, signals cannot travel as effectively. Patients' muscles quit responding to signals from the brain.

Patients who have Guillain-Barré develop a wide variety of symptoms depending on which nerves are affected. Symptoms can include difficulty breathing, weakness in the arms and legs, difficulty swallowing, or trouble with the facial muscles that control eye movement. Initial symptoms are often mild, such as tingling. They grow worse with time. Severely sick patients may be paralyzed, requiring a

HERE TODAY, GONE TOMORROW

Between 2013 and 2014, nearly 20,000 people in the island cluster of French Polynesia fell sick with the Zika virus.[3] The disease reached epidemic levels, but laboratory tests have not confirmed a single case of the virus there since April 2014. Doctors do not know if this means that the virus is gone for good or if the population has developed immunity to it and no one is getting sick enough to seek medical care.

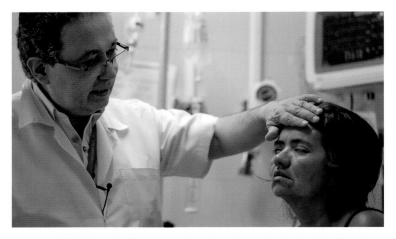

Guillain-Barré affects muscles throughout the body, including those in the face.

ventilator and breathing tube until they can again breathe on their own.

Unlike Zika virus patients, Guillain-Barré patients must be hospitalized. Symptoms can last for weeks or months and are treated in two ways. In the first, doctors remove blood from the patient. The blood is processed to remove both the white and red blood cells. These blood cells are then reinjected into the patient. This is called plasma exchange. Doctors are not certain why it works, but patients who undergo this treatment get well faster than those who do not.

The other treatment for Guillain-Barré syndrome is called immunoglobulin therapy. In this treatment, doctors inject the patient with large doses of proteins. The proteins are the same ones the immune system uses to attack invading infections. These proteins come from healthy donors. The injection makes the immune system's attack on the nervous system less severe, though scientists are not entirely sure how.

The Zika virus outbreak in French Polynesia was the first time Guillain-Barré was linked to the virus. The outbreak was also noteworthy due to the large number of people who were infected. Approximately 28,000 people, 10 percent of the island territory's population, sought medical attention.[4] This was the first epidemic caused by the Zika virus.

STUDYING GUILLAIN-BARRÉ SYNDROME

Doctors are still looking into the causes of Guillain-Barré syndrome. One of the things they are researching is which parts of a patient's immune system are involved in the attack on the nervous system. Doctors suspect there may be proteins in viruses that are similar to proteins on the myelin that lines the body's nerves. Fighting off the virus might then lead the body to see similar myelin proteins as something that should be attacked and destroyed. Researchers hope finding answers will lead to ways to prevent and treat this syndrome.

FROM THE HEADLINES

THE ZIKA VIRUS FAMILY TREE

When scientists want to know how quickly a virus is changing or how closely two strains are related, they look at the sequenced genome of each virus. Scientists recovered fragments of Zika virus RNA from the serum of the patients on Yap Island. They were able to combine these fragments to create an entire genome. The next step was to sequence the virus's genome, creating a complete map of the genetic material. This sequence was then compared to the virus discovered in 1947. This comparison showed the genome of the Yap Island virus was 88.9 percent identical.[5]

Using the information from other sequenced Zika virus genomes, scientists have created a phylogenetic tree of the Zika virus. This is something like a family tree, showing how closely related the viruses from various outbreaks are. Scientists have discovered this tree has two main branches: an African one and an Asian one. This phylogenetic tree can be helpful as scientists work to figure out how the virus spreads into a new area, such as Brazil.

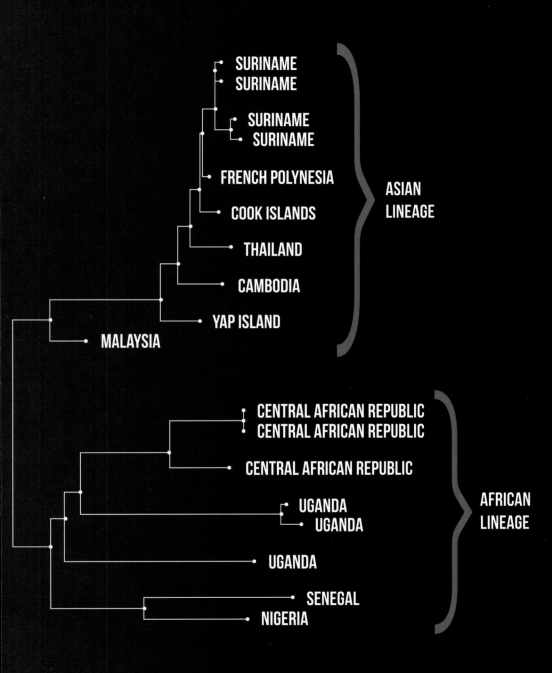

SURINAME
SURINAME
SURINAME
SURINAME
FRENCH POLYNESIA
COOK ISLANDS
THAILAND
CAMBODIA
YAP ISLAND
MALAYSIA

ASIAN
LINEAGE

CENTRAL AFRICAN REPUBLIC
CENTRAL AFRICAN REPUBLIC
CENTRAL AFRICAN REPUBLIC
UGANDA
UGANDA
UGANDA
SENEGAL
NIGERIA

AFRICAN
LINEAGE

CHAPTER FIVE

HOW THE ZIKA
VIRUS MOVES

When people hear about the Zika virus spreading to the island of Yap and then into French Polynesia, it is easy to assume the infected *Aedes* mosquitoes simply flew to these new territories. However, this is not possible. *Aedes* mosquitoes are weak fliers. Female *Aedes aegypti* mosquitoes fly a maximum range of approximately 1,300 feet (400 m).[1] But mosquitoes can migrate without having to fly the distance themselves. Scientists have discovered many animals travel alongside their human hosts. This means insects, such as mosquitoes, that live in close proximity to human beings move to new areas along with traveling people.

Human movement enables the widespread transmission of diseases via mosquitoes.

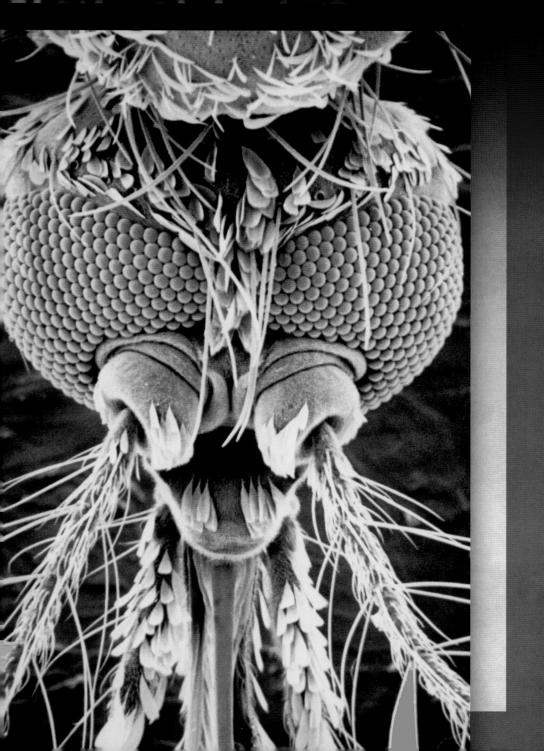

In modern times, mosquitoes travel around the world in cargo airplanes and container ships, but the *Aedes aegypti* mosquito is not a recent migrant. It came to the Americas with European explorers. That is also when yellow fever came to the Americas. The fever was documented on Mexico's Yucatan Peninsula in 1648. Scientists believe *Aedes aegypti* was the vector for the spread of this virus in the Americas.

The question scientists are still trying to answer is whether the *Aedes aegypti* mosquitoes came to the Americas directly from Africa or via Europe. At the time the mosquito arrived in the Americas, Europe was engaged in a triangular pattern of trade. European ships picked up enslaved Africans in west Africa and took them to the Americas. There, the slaves were traded for goods, which were then taken back to Europe. This means the mosquitoes that arrived in the

MODERN MIGRATIONS

The *Aedes aegypti* is not the only *Aedes* mosquito that immigrated to the Americas. *Aedes albopictus* made the trip in the 1980s in a cargo of used tires brought to the United States from China. Commonly known as the Asian tiger mosquito, this mosquito can now be found in many parts of the continental United States. Unlike native mosquitoes, it feeds all day long instead of feeding at only dawn or dusk. The Asian tiger mosquito spreads West Nile virus and also heartworms that affect dogs.

Americas could have come from Africa or from Europe. Whichever path they took, *Aedes aegypti* mosquitoes have since traveled across oceans and around the world thanks to their close association with human beings.

PEOPLE POWERED

The Zika virus does not have to travel from place to place in an infected mosquito. It can make the trip in an infected human being. This happens when a person who has been infected with the virus travels someplace that does not have the virus but does have potential vectors. If this person is then bitten by an *Aedes aegypti* mosquito, or any other mosquito that can be a vector, the mosquito can become infected and pass the virus on to the next person it bites. As the cycle repeats, more mosquitoes become infected and pass the virus on to even

NOT EVERY MOSQUITO IS A DANGER

There are approximately 3,500 mosquito species in the world.[2] So far, only *Aedes aegypti* has been proven to spread the Zika virus. Some mosquitoes never bite people because they feed only on livestock, birds, or lizards. Others may not be threats because they cannot carry the virus. If some types of mosquito bite someone who is infected with the Zika virus, the virus is simply digested along with the mosquito's meal of blood.

more people. The number of infected mosquitoes and people continues growing.

Humans' ability to act as transport systems, moving a virus from place to place, is especially significant given the nature of international travel in today's world. Sporting events, such as the Olympics and the FIFA World Cup, draw teams and spectators, from all over the world. People travel abroad to attend universities. Vacationers fly from continent to continent. Companies do business in multiple countries. Every day, people travel vast distances from one continent to another. Some of them travel to or from Zika-infected areas. Each of these movements creates another opportunity for the virus to spread.

ARRIVING IN YAP

The island of Yap is 800 miles (1,300 km) east of its nearest neighbor, the Philippines. When the virus appeared on Yap, it proved Zika was another virus that could travel great distances, either within a mosquito or in a human host. Health-care professionals still are not certain how the virus made the journey.

In 2016, the city of Rio de Janeiro in Brazil braced for a Summer Olympics in the midst of the Zika threat.

Lieutenant Colonel Mark Duffy, the US Air Force health-care officer assigned to work with doctors in Yap, reported that in July 2007, a medical volunteer working on Yap returned to the United States and then tested positive for Zika antibodies. Duffy did not know whether the infection in Yap came from this person, but the presence of antibodies meant the person had been exposed to the virus.

When asked how far and fast the virus might spread, Duffy hesitated to provide a definite answer. "As an epidemiologist, when you start making predictions about how some of these things are going to behave, they're going to make you look silly every time," Duffy said. "But simply raising concern that there is a potential for it to occur eventually, we felt that was a solid statement that we could stand behind."[3]

WEATHER AND THE ZIKA VIRUS

El Niño is a weather pattern marked by the warming of ocean and coastal waters, typically along the equator. A strong case of it occurred between 2014 and 2016. El Niño affects weather patterns all over the world, raising temperatures and changing rainfall patterns. Some areas that are usually wet will be dry, whereas other areas will have higher-than-normal rainfall and flooding. The *Aedes aegypti* mosquito breeds in standing water. This means El Niño flooding could lead to a rise in the numbers of these mosquitoes, resulting in a faster spread of the virus.

Scientists knew the virus would continue spreading. They just did not know where the next outbreak would be.

SPREADING TO BRAZIL

Brazil had *Aedes aegypti* mosquitoes long before the Zika virus arrived. This left experts trying to figure out how the virus got there. Scientists have sequenced the genetic material in the virus originally found in Uganda. They have also sequenced the viruses from other outbreaks, including those in the Central African Republic, Yap, and French Polynesia. Comparing the sequenced RNA from the Brazilian virus to others shows the strain in Brazil most likely came from French Polynesia. How it got to Brazil remains a mystery, but it was most likely carried from one place to another by an infected person.

"IN THE RIGHT CONDITIONS, WITH SUFFICIENT MOSQUITOES AND CLOSELY PACKED HUMANS, THE VIRUS CAN SPREAD RAPIDLY."[4]

— MARTIN HIBBERD, PROFESSOR OF EMERGING INFECTION DISEASES AT THE LONDON SCHOOL OF HYGIENE AND TROPICAL MEDICINE, DISCUSSING THE RAPID SPREAD OF THE ZIKA VIRUS IN BRAZIL

One theory was that it was carried to Rio de Janeiro, a major Brazilian city that often hosts sporting events. In 2014, the FIFA World Cup, a global soccer championship, was held there. Many health-care experts expected the virus to come over with a competitor, trainer, or fan and make its appearance in Brazil after this competition. But no athletes from any of the infected Polynesian islands attended the event, so it is not the likely source.

The soccer tournament was not the only sporting event that Rio hosted that year. There was also an international canoeing event in August. Competitors from various Pacific islands took part in this event, and some scientists theorized one of these people carried the virus to Brazil. However, scientists found evidence against this theory using sequenced RNA.

As the virus spread, Brazilian researchers worked to determine how and when it had reached their country.

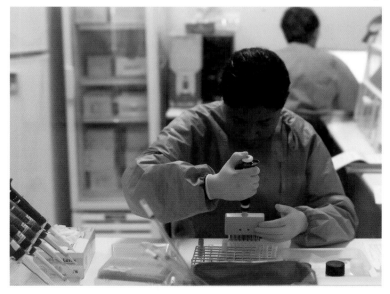

Scientists looked at the RNA of several samples from patients in Brazil. All of the samples looked like each other, suggesting a single person brought the virus to Brazil. This is like what scientists have found in other Zika and dengue outbreaks. But even in similar viruses, the RNA sequences vary slightly from each other because of the rate at which viral RNA evolves. Scientists know what this rate is, and by looking at the various samples, they can calculate how long the virus has been evolving in Brazil. They have calculated it arrived before either the FIFA World Cup or the canoeing tournament. In fact, the virus was in Brazil for approximately a year before any cases were reported. Scientists believe earlier cases were most likely mistaken for dengue or chikungunya.

TRAVELERS BEWARE

Between January 1, 2015, and February 26, 2016, 116 people living in the United States tested positive for the Zika virus. Three-quarters of these people were diagnosed in 2016. They lived in 33 states and Washington, DC.[5] Each of them had traveled to an area where the Zika virus was present or had contact with a traveler who had visited these areas. Haiti, El Salvador, Colombia, Honduras, and Guatemala were the countries most frequently visited. US cases of the Zika virus did not involve people getting bit by a mosquito in the United States. Instead, travelers were infected abroad and returned with the virus.

CHAPTER SIX

MICROCEPHALY
AND BRAZIL

In early 2015, patients in the Brazilian city of Natal sought medical help for what seemed to be infections of the dengue virus. These patients had low fevers, rashes, headaches, and joint pain. A specialist in infectious diseases ran tests and ruled out both the dengue virus and the chikungunya virus.

Reports of patients with similar illnesses came from throughout northeast Brazil. In April, researchers at the Federal University of Bahia discovered the patients had the Zika virus. Additional cases were confirmed in Rio de Janeiro in May. The people of Brazil had never been exposed to this virus before, so they had no immunity. The virus's main insect vector, *Aedes aegypti*, is widespread throughout Brazil. This combination of

In 2015, doctors discovered that the most serious effects of Zika, such as birth defects, appeared in children born to infected mothers.

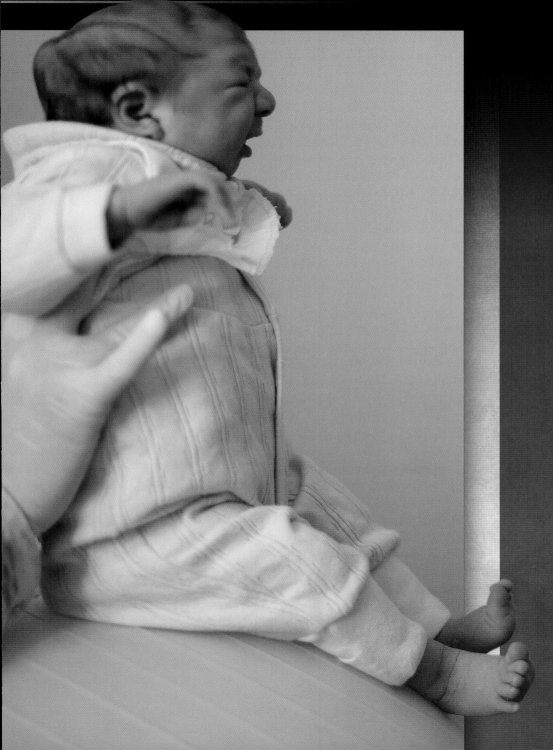

factors allowed the disease to spread rapidly. It was not until the fall of 2015 that Brazilian doctors realized how serious the effects of Zika would be.

BABIES AFFECTED

In October 2015, in the Brazilian state of Pernambuco, 39 babies with smaller than normal brains were born.[1] This condition, called microcephaly, is normally rare. Between January and July of that same year, doctors in the state had delivered only six babies with the condition. This was a typical number for that period. But then August alone saw the birth of six babies with microcephaly, and September followed with 11 more. The number spiked in October.[2] The state's health secretary did not know what could be causing this increase, but he raised an alert and notified Brazil's national government to watch for similar changes elsewhere.

Doctors interviewed the mothers of the babies born with microcephaly. Many of the women had a rash while they were pregnant. They had not been exposed to radiation or pesticide or used alcohol or drugs, all of which could cause microcephaly. The doctors suspected the

Health workers interviewed pregnant women and mothers to learn more about microcephaly's relationship to Zika.

microcephaly was linked to the rash, but they did not have any proof yet that the rash had been caused by the Zika virus. They also did not know whether a pregnant woman could pass the infection on to her baby.

In the fall of 2015, in the state of Para, a baby with microcephaly died very soon after it was born. Doctors found the baby had been infected by the Zika virus. Doctors have since found the virus in the umbilical cords, placentas, livers, lungs, and brains of fetuses with microcephaly that died before birth. The connection between the Zika virus and microcephaly became clear.

MICROCEPHALY

Babies with microcephaly have abnormally small heads at birth because of improper brain development. Because the brain fails to develop, both it and the surrounding skull are smaller than normal. The condition can be the result of genetics. It can also happen if the mother drinks alcohol excessively during pregnancy, is exposed to radiation, or takes certain drugs. Some viral infections, including syphilis, toxoplasmosis, and rubella, are also known to cause it.

In 2014, only 150 babies were born with microcephaly in Brazil. Between October 2015 and January 2016, the number of babies born with the condition was almost 4,000.[3] The increase was greatest in the northeast part of Brazil,

TESTING THE UNBORN

Doctors can often detect signs of Zika virus infection even before a baby is born. In November 2015, a doctor in the state of Paraíba tested the amniotic fluid of two pregnant women. Amniotic fluid surrounds the developing baby, helps it maintain a constant temperature, allows it to move, and provides it with a protective cushion. Both of the women had told their doctors about symptoms that could easily be caused by the Zika virus. Ultrasound images of the developing fetuses had looked normal early in the pregnancies, but one month after the women developed the Zika-like symptoms, ultrasounds showed both fetuses had abnormally small brains. The doctor tested the amniotic fluid of both women and found the Zika virus.

the poorest part of the country, in the states of Paraiba, Pernambuco, and Bahia. In some areas, the ratio of babies born with microcephaly was as high as 1 in 100 live births.[4]

Children who have microcephaly appear visibly different from other infants. Their skulls are smaller than average, so their faces look abnormally large. Although brain and skull growth slows, the skin continues growing. It folds and creases across the skull.

Images of the brains of infants with microcephaly reveal they have calcifications in their brains. This means that calcium, a common mineral in bones, has built up in sections of their brains, causing the brain tissue to harden. Calcification and other brain development issues can result in a variety of symptoms. The children often suffer from tremors or have seizures. They may have tense muscles that are difficult to stretch. Another symptom is hyperreflexia, in which the involuntary nervous system overreacts to various stimuli. This can result in an accelerated heartbeat, sweating, muscle spasms, high blood pressure, and changes in skin color due to blood flow.

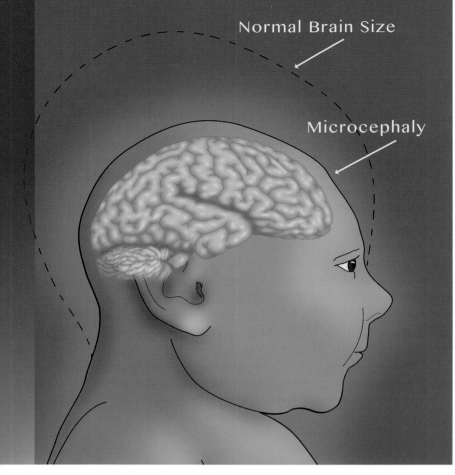

Normal Brain Size

Microcephaly

A reduced brain size can lead to a wide range of neurological problems in children.

But the microcephaly caused by the Zika virus is different than microcephaly from other causes. The neck muscles and muscles of the upper body are unusually stiff in babies who have Zika-induced microcephaly. Another difference is visible in the brain. The human brain is normally covered in ridges and folds. This gives it a high surface area relative to its volume. But in some cases, the brains of babies with Zika virus microcephaly are ridge-free and smooth, like ping pong balls. The damage to the brain is serious enough that trying to help it function normally is impossible. These children will always require special care and assistance.

Doctors are not surprised the Zika virus would cause problems in developing fetal brains. After all, adults who contract the virus may develop neurological problems, such as Guillain-Barré syndrome or a type of brain-swelling called acute disseminated encephalomyelitis (ADEM). In lab mice, the Zika virus causes nerve cells to break down. The brains of the mice also soften. Researchers believe when a woman is infected with the Zika virus early in her pregnancy, the virus infects stem cells crucial for brain development. The virus kills some of the cells and prevents others from dividing. This keeps the brain from developing properly. This ability to damage the brain and nerves, even before birth, means

> "WE'RE NOT AWARE OF ANY MOSQUITO-BORNE DISEASE ASSOCIATED WITH SUCH BIRTH OUTCOMES ON A SCALE ANYTHING LIKE WHAT IS OCCURRING NOW. BECAUSE THE PHENOMENON IS SO NEW, WE ARE QUITE LITERALLY DISCOVERING MORE ABOUT IT EACH AND EVERY DAY."[5]
>
> — TOM FRIEDEN, CDC DIRECTOR, SPEAKING IN APRIL 2016

ZIKA AND ADEM

Two people from Brazil who were infected with the Zika virus later developed a neurological disorder called acute disseminated encephalomyelitis (ADEM). In ADEM, the patient's immune system causes swelling in the brain and spinal cord and damage to the myelin, the protective coating that covers nerve fibers. Patients suffer from weakness, numbness, and loss of both balance and vision. ADEM symptoms typically last for approximately six months. Although scientists believe these two cases of ADEM are associated with the Zika virus, scientists do not yet understand exactly how the virus and the disorder are linked.

the Zika virus can cause significant damage.

The harm this virus does is not limited to the brain development of the infected infant. It also puts stress on Brazilian society and the health care system. The Brazilian government operates and funds the health care, including clinics that provide the therapy needed by children with microcephaly. Due to limited funds and the country's geography, these clinics may be a great distance from where the patient lives. Parents do not pay for the medical treatment, but they may have to pay for a three-hour bus ride to get the child there.

One way to reduce the effect of birth defects is to simply limit the number of pregnancies during a Zika outbreak. However, the Catholic Church has rules against

US health workers from the CDC arrived in Brazil to assist local teams in studying the spread of Zika and its connection with microcephaly.

using birth control, and Brazil is a largely Catholic country. Because of this, it is hard to get birth control. If a woman finds out the fetus she is carrying has microcephaly, she cannot have an abortion. In Brazil, abortion is legal only if the woman was raped, if delivering the baby will kill her, or if the baby has anencephaly, a disorder in which large parts of the brain are missing. With little or no access to birth control or other ways to address this problem, the Zika virus will continue to put a heavy burden on the health-care system of Brazil.

RISK FOR FUTURE PREGNANCIES

Once the Zika virus is no longer in a woman's blood, scientists believe it is safe for her to become pregnant. Because of antibodies in her blood, the woman will be protected from future infection. This may actually help protect the children she carries in future pregnancies.

MORE TO THE
STORY

OTHER BIRTH DEFECTS

Doctors and scientists have noted microcephaly is not the only infant health problem linked to the Zika virus. Occasionally, fetuses simply do not live long enough to be born. Some of them showed signs of microcephaly. Other babies are born with problems such as hearing loss and eye lesions that could lead to blindness. Some are born with arthrogryposis, meaning the infant's joints are stuck in either a flexed or extended position. Still other babies have damaged areas in their brains. "We are extremely concerned . . . this might suggest that [the microcephaly cases] are just the tip of the iceberg," says Dr. Albert Ko from Yale University.[6] Medical issues this serious mean these babies will need care for their entire lives.

CHAPTER SEVEN

FUTURE
CONCERNS

As scientists try to determine where and when a virus might spread, they look at the spread of other viruses. The media does this too, but its comparisons are often less exact. Instead, reporters are often looking for a big story. Because of this, the media often compares the Zika virus to the West Nile virus. Several people in New York City came down with West Nile late in the summer of 1999. No one knew at the time that it was a virus. Patients were coming down with a strange neurological disease that caused encephalitis, seizures, and in some cases even death. W. Ian Lipkin, an expert in viruses working at the University of California, Irvine, identified the virus as the cause when he examined a patient's blood. The virus,

Workers in health department command centers throughout the Americas work to develop responses to contain and eliminate Zika.

spread by the *Culex pipiens* mosquito, had infected people, horses, and a variety of birds, many of which grew sick and died.

Scientists do not look to West Nile when they want to predict where the Zika virus might spread. The West Nile virus is scary and makes for a dramatic story, but it is spread by a different type of mosquito than the one that spreads Zika. To predict where a virus will spread, scientists typically look at what spreads it. By this measure, a much more accurate comparison would be chikungunya, which is spread by the *Aedes aegypti* mosquito as well.

Before 1999, chikungunya was found in Africa, Asia, and India. The number of infections was low until a large 1999–2000 outbreak in the Democratic Republic of the Congo and a 2007 outbreak in Gabon.

WEST NILE AND NATURAL IMMUNITY

Viruses can also take a heavy toll on animal populations with no natural immunity. That is what happened in 1999 and 2000 when the West Nile virus infected horses, crows, and songbirds in the United States. Although many birds recovered from the infection, certain birds, including crows and jays, often died. Horses developed symptoms such as fever, twitching, and aimless wandering. More than 30 percent of infected horses died.[1] Slowly but surely, birds and horses throughout the United States are developing immunity to the disease, but until that happens, the rate of infection will be high.

Workers in chikungunya-affected countries sprayed to kill the mosquitoes that transmit the disease.

The virus spread into Southeast Asia as early as 2006. India, Indonesia, Maldives, Myanmar, and Thailand have reported more than 1.9 million cases.[2] Europe saw its first local transmission of the disease in 2007 with an outbreak in northeastern Italy. The first transmission in the Americas occurred on the Caribbean island of Saint Martin in December 2013, but Puerto Rico is the example that most worries scientists.

In May 2014, the first chikungunya infection was identified in Puerto Rico. By August, approximately 10,000 Puerto Rican cases had been reported. Eventually, one-fourth of the adult population was infected. But the disease did not stop in Puerto Rico. It spread to 45 countries in the Americas. A total of approximately 1.7 million cases, not all confirmed, were reported to the Pan American Health Organization.[3] By 2014, 2,811 cases had been reported in the United States. The vast majority involved people who had traveled and returned to the United States with the infection, but 12 cases of locally transmitted chikungunya have been reported in Florida.[4] The spread in the United States has not been as fast as the spread in Puerto Rico.

AEDES IN THE UNITED STATES

How far and how fast the Zika
virus will spread in the United
States depends largely on
the presence of vectors for
the virus. The *Aedes aegypti*
mosquito already lives in many
southern states, including
Georgia, Florida, and Texas. If
Aedes aegypti mosquitoes are
the only efficient US vectors,
then the geographic spread of
the virus may be limited to the mosquito's range. Without
other vectors, it would not be able to spread to the rest of
the country.

The problem is that there are other *Aedes* mosquitoes
in the United States. The one of greatest concern after
Aedes aegypti is *Aedes albopictus*. Commonly called the
Asian tiger mosquito, *Aedes albopictus* is considered the
most invasive mosquito in the world. This mosquito has
migrated from its native range in Asia and continues to live

POVERTY AND DISEASE

When it comes to viral epidemics,
poverty matters. Although the
wealthy will not completely avoid
getting sick, it is the poor who
will usually be hardest hit. In
part, this is because the poor
are exposed to more mosquitoes.
Their dwellings may lack window
screens to keep insects out.
The poor are also less likely to
seek medical care. Sometimes
this is because they cannot
afford the transportation to a
medical clinic. In some areas of
Brazil, the journey to a clinic for
microcephaly treatments may
require a three-hour drive in
places where many do not have
reliable transportation.

closely with human beings. Like *Aedes aegypti*, it can serve as a vector for the chikungunya virus, but its range within the United States is much larger than that of *Aedes aegypti*. *Aedes albopictus* lives along the Gulf of Mexico and Atlantic Ocean coastlines up to New Jersey and as far inland as Missouri, Kansas, and Oklahoma.

Whether this might worsen the spread of the Zika virus is unknown. In one Singapore study, female *Aedes albopictus* mosquitoes ingested the Zika virus and were then shown to be infected. The virus was present in their saliva, but the study did not determine whether the mosquitoes could easily pass along the infection.

Aedes mosquitoes are not the only potential mosquito vectors that deserve consideration. Scientists working at Fiocruz, Brazil's top biomedical institute, infected *Culex* mosquitoes with the virus. Unlike the *Aedes* mosquitoes, which, like the virus, are originally from Africa, *Culex* mosquitoes are from the Americas. They feed from multiple species, including people, and live in a wide range that stretches from Alaska to Argentina. *Culex pipiens* is the primary mosquito responsible for spreading the

US states encouraged residents to take antimosquito measures, such as draining and covering containers of standing water in which the insects could breed.

Feeling the sting of
mosquitoes?
Then it's time to
drain and cover.

DRAIN

Drain standing water.

Drain water from garbage cans, house gutters, pool

West Nile virus in the United States. But scientists have yet to determine whether it can become infected and act as a Zika vector in the wild. Until studies are done, scientists remain uncertain how far the virus may spread in the Americas.

MONKEY BUSINESS

In Africa and Asia, monkeys can be infected by and carry the Zika virus. In fact, there is a case of a monkey transmitting the virus to a human being. In 2015, a 27-year-old Australian man was traveling in Bali, Indonesia, when a monkey bit him. The man then came down with the virus. Scientists realized from this that Asian monkeys carry the virus in their saliva at high enough levels to transmit it.

After this incident, scientists were still not sure whether the virus could infect South and Central American monkeys. Tamarins, howler monkeys, and squirrel monkeys, all from the Americas, are seldom used in experiments, so their ability to contract African viruses is largely unknown. Scientists have conducted experiments to discover whether American monkeys could contract the dengue virus, which is related to the Zika virus. So far, no American monkeys have been infected. But because of the expense of research animals, attempts have been limited. By early 2016, the possibility of Zika infection in American monkeys remained untested.

BEYOND BLOOD

While scientists research the ways the Zika virus can be transmitted, they are also researching the variety of ways one human being could transmit it to another. Although the virus can be found in blood for only five days, researchers have confirmed it can be transmitted through a blood transfusion. At first, it seemed as though this might not be the case. During the outbreak in French Polynesia, blood donors were tested.

MYSTERIOUS HOWLER MONKEY DIE-OFF

Early in 2016, researchers found 40 dead howler monkeys in the forests of the Central American nation of Nicaragua. The monkeys had no visible injuries or signs of illness. "Wild animals die off all the time, but it is really unusual to see this many deaths in such a short time with no apparent reason. I have never seen anything like it," says conservation researcher Kim Williams-Guillen, who has been researching in Nicaragua since 1999.[5] At the same time, Nicaragua has seen a surge in the number of people contracting the Zika virus. It is too soon to know for certain, but scientists wonder whether there is a connection. They know Howler monkeys are immune to the dengue virus, which suggests they may also be immune to Zika. Until scientists know for certain, they will continue searching for the cause of the die-off.

Approximately 2.8 percent of them were found to have the virus, but there were no reports of the virus being transmitted through an infected transfusion.[6]

That all changed in Brazil. Two patients were found to have the Zika virus following blood transfusions. One, a gunshot victim, later died of his injuries, so no further tests were done to confirm the transfusion was the source of his infection. Genetic sequencing confirmed the other patient was infected through a transfusion from a donor who tested positive for the virus. Scientists are working to assess the public health risk a potentially contaminated blood supply poses.

There is also increasing evidence the Zika virus can be sexually transmitted. This means condom use may be essential to reduce the spread of the virus from men to their partners. The first evidence came in 2008. Two male scientists who had been studying the Zika virus in the African country of Senegal returned to the United States. Both had been infected by the virus but were not showing symptoms yet when they returned to their homes in Colorado. Nine days after the men returned home, one of

Public health agencies launched a campaign to test the blood of pregnant women in Puerto Rico for Zika.

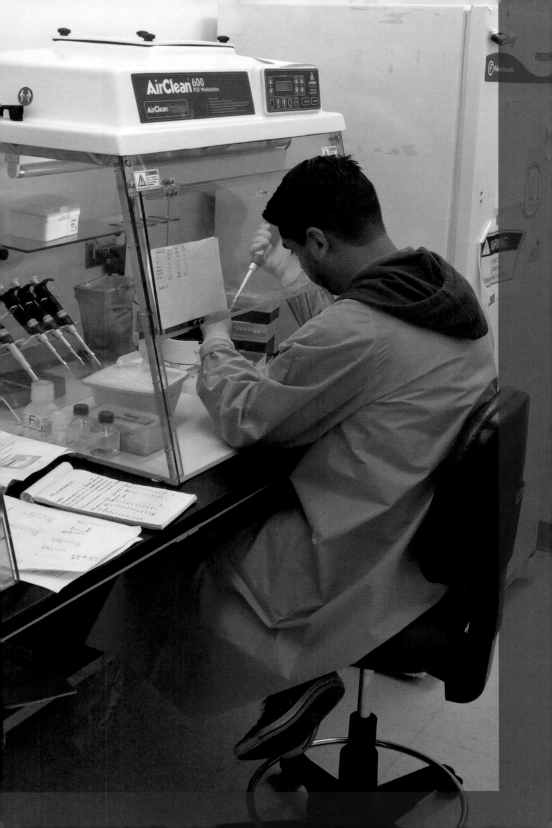

their wives also became sick. Although she tested positive for Zika infection, she had not traveled to either Africa or Asia and had not left the United States since 2007. She had gotten the disease from her husband before he started showing symptoms.

In another instance, a man in the United Kingdom had a fever, exhaustion, and a rash after returning from the Cook Islands in 2014. A Zika outbreak was taking place on the nearby island of Tahiti, part of French Polynesia, so doctors tested his blood. Three days after the onset of his fever, he tested positive for the Zika virus. He was tested several more times to determine how long the virus would remain in his body. In tests done 27 and 62 days after the onset of the fever, his blood and saliva came back negative for Zika.[7] A test of his semen still showed the virus, and it was detected at higher levels than is found in blood.

GLOBAL VIRAL OUTBREAKS

Technology makes it possible for people to travel worldwide. With this travel comes the increased likelihood that arboviruses will continue causing epidemics. "Dengue hit with a vengeance in the '90s. Then we had West Nile in 1999, chikungunya in 2013, and lo and behold, now we have Zika in 2015 and 2016. This is a disturbing, remarkable pattern," said Anthony Fauci, director of the National Institute of Allergy and Infectious Diseases in Bethesda, Maryland.[8]

Scientists have also found the virus in urine. When the outbreak hit French Polynesia in 2013, researchers tested both blood and urine for the virus. The virus could be found in the urine for ten or more days, much longer than it can be found in blood. As with semen, urine samples show the virus at a higher level than it is found in blood.

Scientists still have work to do to determine the danger of these infection pathways and how long people are actually contagious once they develop the virus.

"WE'RE STILL LEARNING MORE ABOUT [THE VIRUS IN] SALIVA AND HOW IT WORKS IN THE BODY."[9]

— TOM FRIEDEN, CDC DIRECTOR, SPEAKING IN APRIL 2016

CHAPTER EIGHT

TAKING
ACTION

E ven as scientists worked to learn more about the Zika virus and how far it might advance around the world, governments and their citizens began wondering how to best protect themselves. City and state governments issued warnings to their citizens on how to reduce the threat of mosquitoes. These instructions involved removing standing water and keeping the insects from getting inside homes.

The best defense against mosquitoes at this time is control—tracking the presence of various mosquitoes and spraying to kill. The responsibility for spraying lies in the hands of a variety of city, town, and county governments. The divisions within these governments that handle these tasks include health departments,

Mosquito larvae mature just below the surface of the water, making standing water a prime breeding ground for these insects.

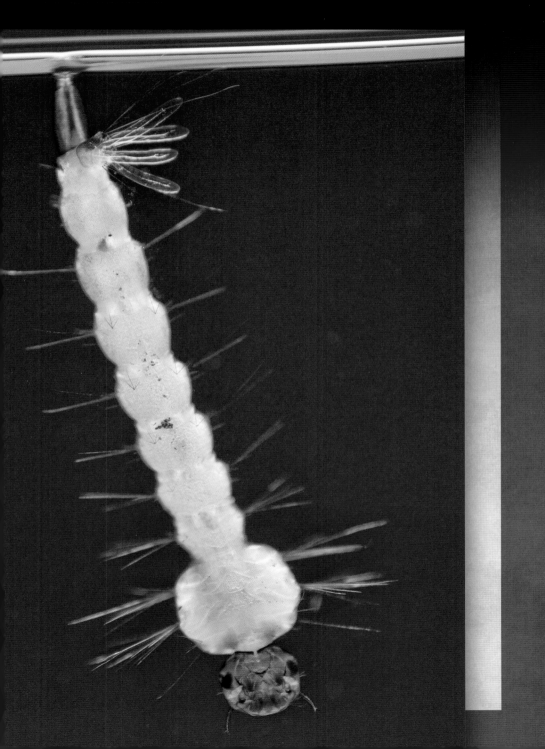

HOME PROTECTION

To reduce the numbers of people who become sick from mosquito-borne illnesses, people need to be safe from mosquitoes when they sleep. Homes should have mesh screens in the windows. If this is not possible, people's beds should be encircled by mosquito nets. People should use mosquito nets even when they nap in the daytime. In addition to keeping the mosquitoes from getting to people, the numbers of mosquitoes need to be reduced. The best way to do this is by taking away the places where they breed. This means getting rid of standing water in buckets, flower pots, and tires, as well as making sure rain barrels are covered. Unfortunately, standing water can be an issue in poor communities, including the areas of Brazil where the Zika virus is a problem. These areas often have no running water. Instead, basins are used to collect water for household use.

transportation agencies, and parks and recreation departments. "There are more than 700 mosquito-abatement districts in the United States, and it can be very difficult to figure out where they fit into public health," says Joseph Conlon, spokesman for the American Mosquito Control Association and former US Navy entomologist.[1]

Not all of these groups have enough funding to do the job well. Most mosquito abatement practices were developed to track and fight the West Nile virus and the *Culex pipiens* mosquitoes. *Aedes aegypti* mosquitoes are active and bite at a different time of day and live in different areas. This means the whole system needs to be reworked to fight the Zika virus.

Workers in New York loaded up a helicopter with larvicide for an airborne antimosquito campaign in June 2016.

One of the top ways to reduce risk from a virus is to vaccinate. Vaccines put small amounts of virus into patients. The virus is either inactive or significantly weakened. The patient's immune system responds to the virus. In doing so, the body develops the antibodies it needs to fight off a live virus if it encounters it in the future.

By 2016, three groups of scientists were working in Brazil to create a Zika virus vaccine. The first group, Bio-Manguinhos, was actually working to develop a vaccine for dengue. Its plan was to use the dengue vaccine as a model to create a vaccine for the Zika virus. Two other groups, one from a company called Butantan and the other at the Evandro Chagas Institute, believed this approach was too complicated. After all, the Zika virus has only one serotype, or strain. The dengue virus has four serotypes. They believed it would be more difficult to create a vaccine that works for four different strains, so they decided to work directly on a Zika vaccine. By July 2016, no vaccine had yet been approved for public use.

Labs animals in the United States are being used to help develop a vaccine. Normally mice cannot be infected by the Zika virus, but researchers at the Washington University School of Medicine in Saint Louis, Missouri, and the University of Wisconsin–Madison School of Veterinary Medicine have developed strains of mice that are not resistant. These mice will be used in the search for a vaccine. Another line of animal research is underway using primates at

ANTIMOSQUITO KITS

Government officials in New York are not sure how high the state's Zika virus risk may be. It depends on which mosquitoes can effectively work as vectors for the virus. These same officials have decided it is better to be safe than sorry, so they are preparing 20,000 antimosquito kits to hand out to women. Each kit includes insect repellent, larvicide tablets to kill young insects in standing water, and educational material. "We want to be prepared. We want to be ahead of it. That's why we're taking aggressive action. We want to do everything we can," said New York governor Andrew Cuomo.[2]

the University of California, Davis, and the University of Wisconsin–Madison. "When we study how the virus affects monkeys, it's very predictive of how it affects people and that information enables us to develop vaccines to fight it," says Koen Van Rompay, one of the University of California researchers.[3] Both teams are exploring how different strains of the virus affect primates. They want to see whether different strains lead to different symptoms. The more scientists learn, the closer they get to a vaccine.

STRUCTURE REVEALED

Purdue University scientists made a discovery that may make creating a vaccine much easier. Using a method called cryo-electron microscopy, these scientists mapped the structure of the Zika virus. To do this, they froze virus particles and then shot electrons through the frozen sample. This created tens of thousands of two-dimensional micrograph images, which are digital photos taken through a microscope or electron microscope. Combined, the images generated a three-dimensional map. The map shows detail down to nearly the atomic level, yielding the clearest picture of this virus yet.

From the map, the scientists discovered the Zika virus looks much like other flaviviruses. The difference lies in one type of protein. The envelope that coats Zika virus particles has 180 of these proteins on it.[4] Scientists believe it is this protein that allows the Zika virus to invade human host cells. The Zika virus is able to cross barriers between the blood and brain. It can also travel through the placenta, which acts as a barrier between the mother and child. Scientists suspect this protein difference may help explain how this unusual feat is possible. Scientists hope this protein will provide the answer for how and why the virus attacks nerve cells. It may also provide clues to why Zika leads to birth defects, such as microcephaly.

"I THINK, WITH THIS, WE'LL BE ABLE TO MAKE A ZIKA VACCINE. BUT YOU NEVER SAY NEVER, AND YOU NEVER SAY ALWAYS."[5]

— ANTHONY FAUCI, DIRECTOR OF THE NATIONAL INSTITUTE OF ALLERGY AND INFECTIOUS DISEASES, ON THE POSSIBILITIES AFTER SCIENTISTS DISCOVERED WHAT THE ZIKA VIRUS LOOKS LIKE

Understanding the structure of the virus may also help researchers create tests to more easily detect it. Part of this means being able to more quickly distinguish a Zika viral infection from a dengue viral infection. Knowledge of the

Studying the Zika virus and its structure in sophisticated laboratories was an early step in learning how to detect it and developing a vaccine.

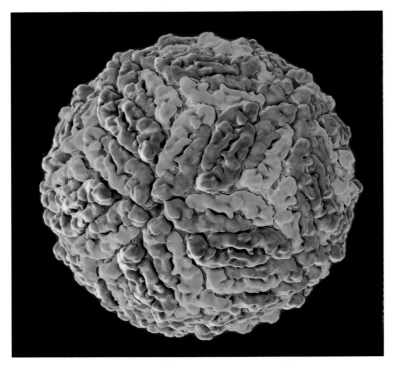

Learning more about the Zika virus's structure will lead to more ways to detect and fight the virus.

Zika virus's protein coating may be the breakthrough that is needed to create a vaccine.

GENETICALLY MODIFIED ORGANISMS

Other scientists are going after the mosquitoes that act as vectors for the virus. Traditionally, people have used chemical sprays to poison mosquitoes. These sprays are sometimes ineffective, and they typically grow less effective with time. Scientists are looking for better means to reduce mosquito populations.

A British biotech firm called Oxitec has genetically modified the *Aedes* mosquito to keep it from being able to reproduce. The scientists at Oxitec insert a gene into the mosquito. This particular gene produces a protein that turns other genes on or off. This ability to stop a gene from functioning kills the mosquitoes before they reach adulthood. In the laboratory, scientists feed mosquitoes that have received the gene an antibiotic called tetracycline. This keeps the protein that blocks the other genes from being produced, and the captive mosquitoes mature and become adults. These mosquitoes, all male, are then released into the wild, where they mate with unmodified mosquitoes. Their offspring have the modified gene. Because the offspring are not fed tetracycline, they produce the protein, which causes them to die.

FOGGING FRUSTRATION

Although many communities around the world spray or fog with pesticides to kill mosquitoes, the WHO has announced that the most commonly used pesticides do not reduce the number of people who contract mosquito-borne diseases. Part of the problem is that although sprays kill some mosquitoes, others are not susceptible and survive the chemical sprays. These mosquitoes then reproduce, and their offspring are also resistant to the pesticides. As the number of resistant mosquitoes in the population grows, the poison kills fewer and fewer of the mosquitoes while running the risk of killing helpful insects, such as bees.

Oxitec has already used this technique to reduce the number of *Aedes aegypti* mosquitoes in various areas of the world, including parts of Brazil, Panama, and the Cayman Islands. In the areas where modified mosquitoes were released, the wild population dropped by more than 90 percent.[6] In March 2016, the US Food and Drug Administration gave preliminary approval to Oxitec to release these modified mosquitoes in Florida.

NOMOREMOS

A company from Saint Louis called Forrest Innovations has a different plan to reduce the mosquito population. In its program, called NoMoreMos, mosquitoes are sterilized at the larval stage. When mosquitoes hatch from eggs, they are called larvae and look very different from adult mosquitoes. Mosquito larvae appear vaguely wormlike and live in water. They molt, or shed their skin, four times

Oxitec's genetically modified mosquitoes may help remove the Zika virus's most important vector.

as they grow. As larvae, female mosquitoes weigh a little more than male mosquitoes. This fact means machines can easily sort the larvae, separating the males and females. A chemical solution is then applied to the male larvae, sterilizing them. The sterile larvae mature normally and can be released into the wild.

Forrest Innovations planned to release 25 million mosquitoes per week from June through August of 2016 in Brazil.[8] The company estimated this would reduce the wild population of mosquitoes by 90 percent in only one season.[9] It had been working in Brazil for several years toward reducing the threat of dengue fever in the country. Because of this, the company already had facilities and equipment set up for working with the mosquitoes. It was able to repurpose existing facilities to work on Zika, rather than having to start from scratch.

Representatives of the company admit some people are concerned about the effect on the environment of drastically reducing the population of *Aedes aegypti* mosquitoes. They claim there is no reason for concern since the mosquitoes are not native to the Americas.

The mosquitoes are not a primary food source for bats and birds.

The more scientists learn about the Zika virus, the closer they get to creating a vaccine and finding ways to combat the mosquitoes that are a vector for the virus. Until then, individuals will have to continue taking the standard steps for fighting mosquito-borne illnesses. They must keep themselves from getting bit and reduce the places where the insects can breed. With smart solutions, people can work together to minimize the effect of the Zika virus.

"OUR TOP PRIORITY WILL BE TO PROTECT PREGNANT WOMEN AND THE DEVELOPING FETUS. WE CAN DO THAT BY—FOR WOMEN IN PARTS OF THE U.S. LIKE PUERTO RICO WHERE ZIKA IS SPREADING—HELPING THEM REDUCE THE LIKELIHOOD THEY WILL GET BITTEN BY AN INFECTED MOSQUITO, AND FOR WOMEN WHO CHOOSE NOT TO GET PREGNANT, INCREASING THEIR ACCESS TO VOLUNTARY EFFECTIVE CONTRACEPTION. RIGHT NOW THAT ACCESS IS VERY LOW IN PUERTO RICO."[10]

— TOM FRIEDEN, CDC DIRECTOR

ESSENTIAL
FACTS

MAJOR EVENTS

- In April 1947, scientists discovered the Zika virus in the Ugandan Zika Forest.

- In 1964, the first human case of the virus was documented when David Simpson, a student studying the virus in a Ugandan lab, got sick.

- In April and May of 2007, the virus infected people on the island of Yap in the Pacific Ocean, marking the first time the virus had been found outside of Africa and Asia.

- In 2013 and 2014, the virus infected people in French Polynesia. For the first time, doctors noted that some patients developed a form of paralysis known as Guillain-Barré syndrome.

- In early 2015, patients in Brazil were found to have the Zika virus. During this outbreak, doctors made the connection between the Zika virus and microcephaly.

KEY PLAYERS

- In 1947, scientists George Dick, Stuart Kitchen, and Alexander Haddow discovered the Zika virus in a sick rhesus monkey and looked for the virus in the blood of human beings and mosquitoes.

- In the United States, the Centers for Disease Control and Prevention (CDC) monitors incidents of the virus, looking for cases of local transmission.

IMPACT ON SOCIETY

Although the Brazilian Zika virus epidemic of 2015 claimed very few lives, the number of infants born with microcephaly raised concerns regarding the lifelong health-care costs for these children. People in the United States feared the spread of this virus. Health-care officials expected it to arrive in the United States, though because it is spread by different mosquitoes than the familiar West Nile virus, the pattern of its spread remained unclear.

QUOTE

"In the right conditions, with sufficient mosquitoes and closely packed humans, the virus can spread rapidly."

—Martin Hibberd, professor of emerging infection diseases at the London School of Hygiene and Tropical Medicine, discussing the rapid spread of the Zika virus in Brazil

GLOSSARY

AUTOIMMUNE DISEASE
An illness in which the body is attacked by its own immune system.

ENDEMIC
Something that is regularly found in a given environment.

ENTOMOLOGIST
A scientist who studies insects.

EPIDEMIC
The rapid spreading of a disease so that many people have it at the same time.

IMMUNITY
Resistance to disease.

NEUROLOGICAL
Of the brain, spinal cord, or nerves.

OUTBREAK

A sudden rise in the occurrence of a disease.

RNA

Ribonucleic acid, the genetic material found in many viruses.

SEQUENCING

The analysis of the order of nucleotides or nucleic acids in genetic material such as RNA or DNA.

SEROTYPE

A distinct variant of a bacteria or virus species, or of immune cells produced in different individuals in response to those pathogens.

SERUM

The water-like component of blood that contains blood cells and disease-fighting antibodies.

VECTOR

An organism, such as an insect, capable of transmitting a virus, bacteria, or other microbial pathogen.

VIRUS

A microscopic particle coated in protein that can reproduce only by infecting another organism and hijacking cells within that organism.

ADDITIONAL
RESOURCES

SELECTED BIBLIOGRAPHY

Ayres, Constancia F. J. "Identification of Zika Virus Vectors and Implications for Control." *The Lancet.* March 2016. PDF.

Cauchemez, Simon, et al. "Association between Zika virus and Microcephaly in French Polynesia, 2013–2015." *The Lancet.* March 2016. PDF.

Hayes, Edward B. "Zika Virus Outside Africa." *Emerging Infectious Diseases* 15.9 (2009): 1347–1350. Print.

FURTHER READINGS

Hand, Carol. *Epidemiology: The Fight Against Ebola & Other Diseases.* Minneapolis, MN: Abdo, 2015. Print.

Laine, Carolee. *Ebola Outbreak.* Minneapolis, MN: Abdo, 2016. Print.

Piddock, Charles. *Outbreak.* Washington, DC: National Geographic, 2008. Print.

WEBSITES

To learn more about Special Reports, visit **booklinks.abdopublishing.com**. These links are routinely monitored and updated to provide the most current information available.

FOR MORE INFORMATION

For more information on this subject, contact or visit the following organizations:

Centers for Disease Control and Prevention
1600 Clifton Road
Atlanta, GA 30329-4027
800-232-4636
http://www.cdc.gov/zika/
This US health organization has an extensive website on the Zika virus and the latest findings as well as travel advisories and statistics on the virus in the United States.

World Health Organization
Avenue Appia 20
1211 Geneva 27
Switzerland
+ 41 22 791 21 11
http://www.who.int/mediacentre/factsheets/zika/en/
The WHO provides information about Zika's history and scientific background, as well as information about the group's response to the disease.

SOURCE NOTES

CHAPTER 1. TAKING ZIKA SERIOUSLY

1. Jade Coelho de Miranda. "'I Ached and My Hands Felt Frozen': A Zika Virus Victim's Tale." *New York Post*. New York Post, 28 Jan. 2016. Web. 30 Mar. 2016.

2. Austin Ramzy. "Experts Study Zika's Path from First Outbreak in Pacific." *New York Times*. New York Times, 10 Feb. 2016. Web. 28 July 2016.

3. Steven Reinberg. "How Likely Are Birth Defects from Zika Virus? New Study Finds Clues." *CBS News*. CBS News, 16 Mar. 2016. Web. 28 July 2016.

4. Laurie Garrett. "The Zika Virus Isn't Just an Epidemic. It's Here to Stay." *Foreign Policy*. Foreign Policy, 28 Jan. 2016. Web. 28 July 2016.

5. Margaret Chan. "WHO Director-General Addresses Media after Zika Emergency Committee." *World Health Organization*. WHO, 8 Mar. 2016. Web. 28 July 2016.

6. Maya Wei-Haas. "How Can Viruses Like Zika Cause Birth Defects?" *Smithsonian Magazine*. Smithsonian, 4 Feb. 2016. Web. 28 July 2016.

7. Ann M. Powers. "Overview of Emerging Arboviruses." *Future Virology* 2009: 391–401. Web. 19 Apr. 2016.

8. "Where Has Chikungunya Virus Been Found?" *CDC*. CDC, 12 May 2016. Web. 28 July 2016.

9. Dileep Mavalankar, et al. "Increased Mortality Rate Associated with Chikungunya Epidemic, Ahmedabad, India." *Emerging Infectious Diseases* 2008: 412–415. Web. 28 July 2016.

10. Michaeleen Doucleff. "Painful Virus Sweeps Central America, Gains a Toehold in the US." *NPR*. NPR, 1 Jan. 2015. Web. 19 Apr. 2016.

CHAPTER 2. WHAT IS ZIKA?

1. Keith Wagstaff. "Aedes Aegypti: Why One Mosquito Is So Good at Spreading the Zika Virus." *Forbes*. Forbes, 11 Feb. 2016. Web. 12 Apr. 2016.

2. "Fact Sheet for Patients." *CDC*. CDC, 26 Feb. 2016. Web. 28 July 2016.

3. Anne Trafton. "A New Paper-Based Test for the Zika Virus." *MIT News Office*. MIT, 6 May 2016. Web. 27 May 2016.

4. Julie Steenhuysen. "US Moms-to-Be to Seek Reassurance about Zika after Trips Abroad." *Reuters*. Reuters, 25 Jan. 2016. Web. 28 July 2016.

CHAPTER 3. DISCOVERING ZIKA

1. Edward B. Hayes. "Zika Virus outside Africa." *Emerging Infectious Diseases*. CDC, Sept. 2009. Web. 28 July 2016.

2. Justin Rowlatt. "Why Asia Should Worry about Zika Too." *BBC News*. BBC News, 2 Feb. 2016. Web. 28 July 2016.

3. "Zika Virus: Inside Uganda's Forest where the Disease Originates." *BBC News*. BBC News, 29 Jan. 2016. Web. 28 July 2016.

CHAPTER 4. GUILLAIN-BARRÉ AND FRENCH POLYNESIA

1. "Zika Virus: Key Facts." *World Health Organization*. WHO, Jan. 2016. Web. 28 July 2016.

2. Jason Beaubien. "Zika in French Polynesia: It Struck Hard in 2013, Then Disappeared." *NPR*. NPR, 9 Feb. 2016. Web. 11 Apr. 2016.

3. Ibid.

4. Austin Ramzy. "Experts Study Zika's Path from First Outbreak in Pacific." *New York Times*. New York Times, 10 Feb. 2016. Web. 28 July 2016.

5. Ned Hayes. "Zika Virus Outbreak on Yap Island." *International Society for Infectious Diseases*. International Society for Infectious Diseases, 2009. Web. 28 July 2016.

CHAPTER 5. HOW THE ZIKA VIRUS MOVES

1. "WHO: Zika Virus and Potential Complications: Questions and Answers." *World Health Organization*. WHO, 28 Mar. 2016. Web. 29 Mar. 2016.

2. Keith Wagstaff. "Aedes Aegypti: Why One Mosquito Is So Good at Spreading the Zika Virus." *Forbes*. Forbes, 11 Feb. 2016. Web. 12 Apr. 2016.

3. Austin Ramzy. "Experts Study Zika's Path from First Outbreak in Pacific." *New York Times*. New York Times, 10 Feb. 2016. Web. 28 July 2016.

4. Bahar Gholipour. "Zika Virus Was in Brazil a Year before It Was Detected." *LiveScience*. LiveScience, 24 Mar. 2016. Web. 23 Apr. 2016.

5. Sarah G. Miller. "Over 100 Zika Cases Confirmed in US, CDC Says." *LiveScience*. LiveScience, 18 Mar. 2016. Web. 29 Mar. 2016.

SOURCE NOTES
CONTINUED

CHAPTER 6. MICROCEPHALY AND BRAZIL

1. MG Teixeira, et al. "The Epidemic of Zika Virus-Related Microcephaly in Brazil: Detection, Control, Etiology, and Future Scenarios." *American Journal of Public Health* Apr. 2016: 601–605. Web. 28 July 2016.

2. Ibid.

3. "Brazil Zika Outbreak: More Babies Born with Birth Defects." *BBC*. BBC, 21 Jan. 2016. Web. 13 Apr. 2016.

4. Ibid.

5. Lena H. Sun. "CDC's Advice on Zika: You May Need to Consider Avoiding Sex." *Washington Post*. Washington Post, 5 Feb. 2016. Web. 14 Apr. 2016.

6. Lulu Garcia-Navarro. "Zika-Linked Brain Damage in Infants May Be 'Tip of the Iceberg.'" *NPR*. NPR, 29 Jan. 2016. Web. 28 July 2016.

CHAPTER 7. FUTURE CONCERNS

1. "West Nile Encephalomyeletis in Horses." *Merck Manuals*. Merck, 2011. Web. 26 Apr. 2016.

2. "Chikungunya Fact Sheet." *World Health Organization*. WHO, Apr. 2016. Web. 28 July 2016.

3. Maggie Fox. "How Will Zika Spread? Look at Chikungunya, CDC Head Says." *NBC News*. NBC News, 10 Feb. 2016. Web. 26 Apr. 2016.

4. "Chikungunya Virus: 2014 Final Date for the United States." *CDC*. CDC, 30 Oct. 2015. Web. 26 Apr. 2016.

5. Wei-Chih Chang and Kara Sewalk. "Could Zika Be the Mysterious Killer of Howler Monkeys in Nicaragua?" *Disease Daily*. Disease Daily, 24 Feb. 2016. Web. 28 July 2016.

6. "Zika Virus: Transmission and Risks." *CDC*. CDC, 15 Apr. 2016. Web. 26 Apr. 2016.

7. Barry Atkinson, et al. "Detection of Zika Virus in Semen." *Emerging Infectious Diseases Journal*. CDC, May 2016. Web. 28 July 2016.

8. Meghan Rosen. "Rapid Spread of Zika Virus Raises Alarm: Disease Linked to Birth Defect Is Pushing Northward from Brazil." *Science News*. Science News, 20 Feb. 2016. Web. 28 July 2016.

9. Lena H. Sun. "CDC's Advice on Zika: You May Need to Consider Avoiding Sex." *Washington Post*. Washington Post, 5 Feb. 2016. Web. 14 Apr. 2016.

CHAPTER 8. TAKING ACTION

1. Maryn McKenna. "Disorganized Mosquito Control Will Make US Vulnerable to Zika." *National Geographic*. National Geographic, 29 Feb. 2016. Web. 28 July 2016.

2. Megan McGibney. "Cuomo's Zika Protection Plan Includes Condoms and Bug Spray." *New York Post*. New York Post, 18 Mar. 2016. Web. 27 Apr. 2016.

3. Frankie L. Tull. "Zika Virus Vaccine Possible with Help of Primate Research." *Newsweek*. Newsweek, 13 May 2016. Web. 28 July 2016.

4. "Zika Virus Structure Revealed." *NIH Research Matters*. National Institutes of Health, 12 Apr. 2016. Web. 28 July 2016.

5. Rachel Feltman. "Zika's Structure Has Been Revealed, Bringing Scientists Closer to a Vaccine." *Washington Post*. Washington Post, 31 Mar. 2016. Web. 15 Apr. 2016.

6. Chris Creese. "Press Release: Expansion of Oxitec's Vector Control Solution in Brazil Attacking Source of Zika Virus and Dengue Fever after Positive Program Results." *Oxitec*. Oxitec, 19 Jan. 2016. Web. 15 Apr. 2016.

7. Alexandra Sifferlin. "Why America's Top Health Official Is Worried about Zika." *Time*. Time, 21 Apr. 2016. Web. 25 Apr. 2016.

8. Blythe Bernhard. "Local Company Sterilizing Mosquitoes to Fight Zika Virus." *St. Louis Post-Dispatch*. St. Louis Post-Dispatch, 15 Mar. 2016. Web. 29 Mar. 2016.

9. Ibid.

10. Alexandra Sifferlin. "Why America's Top Health Official Is Worried about Zika." *Time*. Time, 21 Apr. 2016. Web. 25 Apr. 2016.

INDEX

immune system, 6, 9, 23, 26, 45, 47, 68, 89

immunoglobulin therapy, 46–47

international travel, 15, 41, 50–54, 59, 84

malaria, 6

microcephaly, 62–71, 77, 93

monkeys, 7, 19, 30, 80–81, 91

mosquitoes
  Aedes aegypti, 19–22, 34, 35, 37, 43, 50–53, 56, 57, 60, 74, 77–78, 88, 96, 98
  Aedes africanus, 21, 33, 37
  Aedes albopictus, 21, 52, 77–78
  Aedes hensilli, 41
  Culex pipiens, 74, 78, 88

Natal, Brazil, 60

nerves, 6, 45, 47, 67–68, 93

New York City, 72, 90

Nigeria, 35, 49

Oxitec, 95–96

Pernambuco, Brazil, 62, 65

Puerto Rico, 76, 99

ribonucleic acid (RNA), 16–18, 38, 48, 57, 59

Rio de Janeiro, Brazil, 4, 57, 60

Simpson, David, 34–35

Southeast Asia, 8, 36–37, 43, 49, 76

sporting events, 54, 57–58

Tahiti, 42, 44, 84

Tanzania, 11, 35

Uganda, 7, 30, 33–34, 37, 49, 57

United States, 13, 52, 56, 59, 74, 76–80, 82, 84, 88, 90, 96

vectors, 18–21, 22, 33, 37, 41, 52–53, 60, 77–80, 90, 94, 99

virus replication, 16–18

weather patterns, 56

West Nile virus, 13, 18, 21, 52, 72–74, 78, 84, 88

World Health Organization, 9, 10, 15, 95

World War II, 43

Yap Island, 8, 38, 41, 42, 44, 48

yellow fever, 6, 13, 18, 21, 30–33, 52

Zika Forest, 7, 30

Zika virus
  blood transmission, 81–82
  diagnosis, 25–28
  discovery, 7, 30–33
  mosquito transmission, 50–53, 77–80
  outbreaks, 11–12, 41, 47, 48, 57, 81, 84–85
  phylogenetic tree, 48–49
  sexual transmission, 82–85
  structure, 91–94
  symptoms, 23–25
  vaccine, 89–91

ABOUT THE
AUTHOR

Sue Bradford Edwards writes nonfiction for children and teens, working from her home in Saint Louis, Missouri. She studied archaeology and history in college. Her writing covers a range of topics, including history and science.